Anthurium scherz(
Araucara excelsa
Asparagus falcatu\
Asparagus meyeri
Asparagus sprengei.
Asparagus phumosus nanus
Aspidistra elatior
Asplenium nidus avis
Begonias of *various flowering varieties*
Begonia masoniana
Begonia rex
Caladium bicolor
Chamaedora elegans *Neanthe bella*
Chlorophytum comosum
Cissus antarctica
Codiaeum *in variety (Crotons)*
Coffea arabica
Cordyline terminalis *Dracaena terminalis*
Cyperus alternifolius
Cyperus diffusus
Cyperus haspan
Cyperus papyrus
Dieffenbachia *various varieties, including,*
   Tropic Snow, Compacta, Perfecta
   compacta, oerstedii, yenmanii, amoena,
   Pia
Dichorisandra reginae
Dizygotheca elegantissima *Aralia*
   elegantissima
Dracaena deremensis 'Warneckei'
Dracaena deremensis 'Souvenir de Schryver'
Dracaena deremensis 'Yellow Stripe'
Dracaena deremensis 'White Stripe'
Dracaena fragrans
Dracaena godseffiana 'Florida Beauty'
Dracaena marginata
Dracaena massangeana
Dracaena Rededge *Baby Doll*
Euphorbia tirucalli
Euphorbia trigona
Euterpe edulis
Fatsia japonica *syn. Aralia sieboldii*
Ficus altissima
Ficus australis
Ficus benghalensis
Ficus benjamina
Ficus buxifolia
Ficus elastica
Ficus elastica decora
Ficus exotica
Ficus krishnae
Ficus lyrata
Ficus nuda
Ficus pandurata
Ficus pumila
Ficus robusta
Ficus schryveriana
Ficus stricta
Ficus triangularis
Fittonia argyroneura
Fittonia Mini *F. nana*
Gynura aurantiaca
Heptapleurum arboricolum hayatii
Heptapleurum arboricolum Geisha Girl
Heptapleurum arboricolum *Schefflera*
   arboricola
Hibiscus rosa-sinensis *in variety*
Hibiscus cooperi

.a var.
   teriana *Kentia forsteriana*
   coneura massangeana *this*
   difficult in hydroculture, unless
   .eal conditions — mainly semi-
   shade
Microcoelum weddelianum *formerly Cocos*
   weddeliana
Mimosa pudica *Sensitive Plant*
Monstera deliciosa *Philodendron pertusum*
Musa cavendishii *nana*
Nephrolepis *in variety — particularly*
   'Boston'. 'Rooseveltii', 'Teddy Junior',
   'Whitmanii' and 'Fluffy Ruffles'
Pachypodium lameri
Pandanus veitchii
Peperomias *in variety, particularly*
   magnoliaefolia, caperata, argyreaus,
   scandens, hederaefolia etc.
Philodendrons *in a multitude of varieties.*
   All Philodendrons with adventitious
   roots are particularly suited to
   hydroculture
P. bipinnatifidum
P. erubescens
P. hastatum
P. ilsemannii
P. laciniatum
P. melanochrysum
P. panduraeforme
P. radiatum
P. Red Emerald
P. scandens
P. squamiferum
P. tuxla
P. selloum
Phoenix canariensis
Phoenix roebelinii
Pilea cadieria
Pilea Bronze
Pilea Moon Valley
Pleomele thalioides
Platycerium alcicorne
Rhaphidophora aurea *previously*
   Scindapsus aureus
Rhaphidophora Marble Queen *previously*
   Scindapsus Marble Queen
Rhoeo discolor
Rhoicissus capensis
Rhoicissus rhomboidea
Rhoicissus rhombifolius Ellen Danica
Saintpaulia ionantha
Sansevieria trifasciata laurentii *and all*
   varieties, including Moonshine,
   Futurata, Flandria
Schefflera actinophylla
Schefflera arboricola
Scirpus cernuus
Setcreasea purpurea
Spathiphyllum Mauna Loa
Spathiphyllum wallisii
Streptocarpus
Syngonium podophyllum
Syngonium podophyllum albonineatum
Tetrastigma voinerianum
Tradescantias *in many varieties*
Yucca elephantipes

Hydroculture

Hydroculture
Indoor Plants on Tap

FRANS DE BRUIJN

London: W. Foulsham & Co Ltd
New York Toronto Capetown Sydney

W. Foulsham & Co Ltd
Yeovil Road Slough Berks England

© HELMOND, B. V., The Netherlands
© 1978 W. FOULSHAM & CO Ltd, Great Britain (English edition)

Pictures on pages 10, 38 & 43
by kind permission of
ROCHFORD LANDSCAPE LTD.

ISBN 0—572—00975—5

Typeset by Preface Ltd, Salisbury
Printed in Great Britain by
A. Wheaton & Co Ltd, Exeter

Contents

The natural texture and colour of this trough ensures that it will harmonise with the traditional decorative atmosphere in which it sits.

Water instead of earth

A striking development of the last few years, possibly resulting from environmental problems, has been that many more people have begun consciously or unconsciously to appreciate trees, culinary herbs and the flowers of the roadside, as well as plants grown indoors and in the garden. Plant collecting, flower arranging and gardening, indoors and out, are popular leisure activities. Housewives, office and factory workers (not to mention the directors) want to be surrounded by greenery of all kinds.

Green is essential, not only out of doors—plants and flowers are great creators of atmosphere in the home. A house, office or working area looks bare without plants and does not make a pleasant environment. Decoration is increasingly provided by such large, showy plants as palms, the larger varieties of ficus, freakishly shaped yuccas and long-stemmed dracaenas, or mixed arrangements in troughs, scattered around the room, rather than plants lined up along the window sill. A tranquil atmosphere may be conjured up with subtle positioning of plants.

It has become evident that even the use of greenery and the treatment of flowers are subject to changes in fashion. We are gradually coming to regard greenery as an essential feature of a healthy living and working environment. Apart from the aesthetic and decorative value of large plants, the contribution that they make to the surrounding climate should be remembered. By releasing moisture into the atmosphere, they help to offset the drying effects of central heating which can make rooms so unpleasant to live and work in, and in offices where calculators and typewriters are constantly rattling a generous screen of plants will deaden the sound.

Considerable expenditure will be involved in purchasing a trough arrangement of suitable size for a large building, like a hospital, and a single imposing plant is little cheaper. It is therefore reasonable to consider the care and treatment necessary for the plants to give lasting pleasure.

Before filling a trough with plants that may have originated in completely different parts of the world, you should ensure that their

What would this room look like without its splendid arrangement of greenery?

needs are compatible. Position and food requirements can both give rise to problems. Consider the plants' natural surroundings. Plants from a shady, humid environment (such as African Violets, Philodendrons or Hoya) will not team happily with others (like Cacti, Aloes or some species of Euphorbia) that are adapted to withstand drought. If you look at the position in which you want the plants to stand, you should find plenty of varieties which will like the conditions you can give them. A Cast Iron Plant (*Aspidistra elatior*), Rubber Plant (*Ficus elastica*) and other kinds of Ficus, *Sansevieria trifasciata* and many types of palm are tolerant and will flourish attractively even when the light is poor and humidity low.

Unless your display of greenery is cared for correctly, many plants will fail to grow and flower, or even worse may die. The right treatment depends on a sensitivity to the reactions of the plant, a living organism, to its environment, so find out all you can about the plants you have chosen and spend time on getting to know them; then you will spot the signs of any trouble before it gets to be a disaster. General rules are often difficult to give and, even then, can only serve as a rough guide. For example, water requirements will depend on the size of the individual plant, its rate of growth, the temperature and brightness of its position, as well as any special demands of the group it belongs to.

The problems of caring for plants in offices are that much greater—who is to look after them at weekends and holiday periods? They are often left to their fate. That fate may be worse than the workers in an office realize. Sometimes the heating is turned off when the office is empty, and in other cases the temperature may rise; either way the plants will have to put up with an unwelcome change. Air conditioning may be turned off, or windows may be left open despite changes in the weather, and the benefit of artificial lighting may be missing.

A view through two rooms which rely heavily on Hydroculture for decoration. Even used individually, these floor standing troughs create great impact. Grouped together they can solve all kinds of problems — dividing a room for example.

Indoor plants living in water

The plants that flourish in the windows of every house are generally potted in earth. That is what we are accustomed to. However, normal indoor plants can live and grow quite differently—in water.

Hydroculture, or water culture, refers to the cultivation of plants by various methods which do not make use of earth or compost. We know that plants do not depend for life on the earth itself, but on the substances it holds, water-soluble chemicals and elements which the plant can absorb. Given support for the roots, and water containing the right nutrients in balanced quantities, the plants can thrive without earth.

An unnatural situation, you may think. That is undoubtedly true, but indoor plants have not simply evolved naturally; they are cultivated to provide human beings with the greenery they need in places where they live and work. The ever increasing demand for greenery in the home led to a search for some means of cultivation which will provide plants with their best chance of life with the minimum of care.

Hydroculture could be the answer.

Above, they grow in soil.

Below, they grow in water.

Historical survey

People have been tilling the earth for thousands of years. They generally colonized areas where good earth was supplied with water, where life was relatively easy for man, the other animals and plants alike.

In ancient times, some consideration was already being given to such work as preparation of the earth, organic fertilizers and irrigation—tasks that were performed mainly by women. Until about 125 years ago, cultivation was dependent only on practical experience. People could see with their own eyes how their efforts encouraged plants to grow and flourish. It was possible to gather the harvest, and so to eat, without any realization that good growth is impossible without a reasonable supply of water and air in the soil, as well as feeding materials which undergo a process of mineral conversion before being taken up by the roots.

Suspicions about the plants' requirements had been aroused very early by the atom hypothesis of the Greek philosopher, Democritus of Abdera, who had believed in about 400 B.C. that all materials are composed of atoms which differ from one another in type and cannot be divided or changed. The nature of a particular material depends on the number and type of the atoms it contains. On the basis of this theory, Nicolas Cusa (1402-46), a priest and scientist, supposed that plants absorb atoms from the earth in order to develop. Most other experimenters between 1400 and 1650 were convinced that water was the only source of food for plants.

An experiment that became a legend

In the neighbourhood of Brussels lived a country nobleman, Jean Baptiste Van Helmont (1577-1644), the discoverer of a number of gases (the word 'gas' originated with him). Hoping to identify the factor that causes plants to thrive, Van Helmont devised an experiment that has since become famous.

He planted a small willow tree, weighing 5 lbs., in a barrel containing 200 lbs. of earth, closing the barrel so that no additional matter could enter, and gave nothing but water for five years. At the end of this water-feeding, Van Helmont removed the tree and found that it weighed 169 lbs. Because the barrel still held 200 lbs. of earth—give or take a few ounces that he put down to experimental error—Van Helmont concluded that the willow tree had grown on water alone.

But if water were the only requirement for the growth of plants, there would be few problems in feeding them.

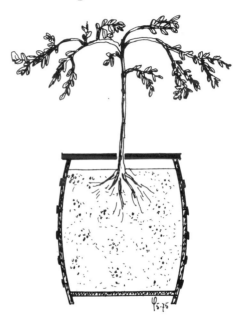

A willow tree (5lb weight) shut in a barrel with 200 lb earth.
An experiment carried out by Jean Baptiste Van Helmont (1577-1644)

Hydroculture troughs can provide decorative impact.

Two ways of growing plants by Hydroculture. On the left, several plants in an earthenware trough. On the right, one of the most modern types of container.

First application of water culture

The Irish investigator, Robert Boyle (1627-91), repeated Van Helmont's experiment and achieved the same results. Boyle, however, accepted the atom hypothesis of Democritus of Abder1, with the difference that he believed in transmutation (the changing of one element into another) by which he envisaged atoms becoming plant tissues. He saw water as an element that would be transmuted into a fertilizer, saltpetre for example. Boyle examined his theory with the help of water culture, and he was the first to put the method into practice. Indeed, in the years 1663-65 he wrote that different land plants grew reasonably well in water. He regarded that as a confirmation of his suppositions about transmutation. Later on, possibly influenced by the work of Glauber (1604-68) and John Mayo (1643-79) who proved that more elements were indispensable to the plant, Boyle wrote that a plant cannot grow on clear rain water alone.

John Woodward, experimenting in England at the end of the seventeenth century, added samples of garden soil to the water in which he was growing plants and concluded from his results that development was improved by substances contained in the soil. Later, important research carried out in France by Nicolas de Saussure in the early nineteenth century and Jean Boussingault in the 1850s helped to identify some of the elements necessary for plant growth. However, it was the experiments of Wilhelm Knop (1817-1910) and Julius von Sachs (1832-1907), who both used water culture in a conscious investigation of the elements essential to plants and of the most favourable quantities and ratios, which served as a starting point for the development of artificial fertilizers.

Application on a commercial scale

A sprig off a neighbour's plant or a cutting from Grannie's lovely fuschia which root in water, or a hyacinth gleaming in a glass of water at Christmas, are all familiar experiments in hydroculture, but in general water culture was for many years restricted to the laboratory. No-one dared to try the method commercially until 1929, when an American professor, W. F. Gericke, put early research to use by growing tomatoes on a commercial basis in California.

He had found that while tomatoes grown in earth occasionally produced a yield that was far above average, even in as favourable a climate as that of California the maximum yield did not seem to be attainable every time. Dr Gericke put this down to nutrient deficiencies in the fertilizers that were used for cultivation in the earth. He thought that water culture (for which he invented the term 'hydroponics') would make it possible to provide plants with every necessary nutrient without any losses. When applied in earth, food substances may be rinsed away, attach themselves to soil particles, or join with other chemicals in forming insoluble compounds, so that it is difficult to gauge how much food is available to the plants. Unfortunately, not enough was known at the time about plant feeding to achieve good results. Difficulties included the use of far too high a concentration of salts in the food solution and insufficient appreciation of the plants' precise iron requirements. Lack of oxygen at the roots was probably another factor leading to less than satisfactory results.

Since 1934, many attempts have been made throughout the world to put soilless cultivation into practice, often with the aim of producing higher yields or later on, in areas where the earth is poor or water scarce, to create the right conditions for growing fresh vegetables. These have nearly always been trials on a let's-see-if-it-works basis, without sufficient knowledge of plant foods or research into the deeper questions of optimum growth, and without any thought of whether there was a real commercial need.

Modern-day alchemists have earned high rewards for advice and information on soilless cultivation in infertile areas, especially in underdeveloped countries. The result has often been failure, but may partly explain the amazing claims which have appeared in newspapers. So, they allege, one square metre of plants grown without earth would be enough to provide a family of four with fresh vegetables for a year! All the Science Fiction treatment made serious researchers more careful. Soilless cultivation, while not often mentioned in the scientific journals, became one science subject that could always find a ready market in the papers. On 31st January a daily in The Hague raved 'Hydroponics: the magic garden for everybody, soup for the plants, granules instead of earth. Do you want to win prizes for the best fruit? Then get to work with the water today. No more dirty hands, no more aching back. Horticulture with kid gloves on . . . and ready while you wait.'

Research by T.N.O.

In 1948, Dr Jan Al, then director of the general technical department of the Dutch organization for Applied Scientific Research (Toegepast Natuurwetenschappelijk Onderzoek—T.N.O.) was of the opinion that, in spite of all failures and disappointments, worthwhile hydroculture research must be possible. After World War II, growers had run into difficulties with a vascular disease that attacked carnations. Even after sterilization of the earth by intensive steaming, the infection persisted in the subsoil and often returned within the year. T.N.O. examined whether it was possible to grow carnations in gravel instead of earth. The first experiments had not been a success. American researchers into gravel culture found that the mould causing the vascular disease spread faster in gravel than in earth. In the Dutch system, however, the disease did not stand a chance because of a food solution developed by T.N.O.

In the ensuing years, extensive research was carried out, particularly in the area of nutrition, but also on oxygen requirements and supply. The research led to a better knowledge of the principal differences between cultivation in earth and water. In 1953, T.N.O. were able to grow carnations in gravel, free of virus infection and with a flower yield equal to that achieved with cultivation in earth. The quality of stems and flowers was definitely higher in winter.

In practice, however, another answer had been found: cultivation in troughs which contained earth in a quantity that could easily be sterilized or replaced, cutting out the risk of reinfection from the subsoil. Gravel culture for carnations therefore came to nothing at that time. The considerable investment then needed for its installation proved a great deterrent for growers. Since the carnation

Plants create an atmosphere.

research had been carried out mainly by the growers themselves, it was evident that, while small changes in growing methods are immediately acceptable, greater upheavals, like the change from earth to gravel, have been greeted with more trepidation when there has been no practical success to justify the risks involved.

In the period 1953-58 and afterwards, T.N.O. investigated the cultivation of flowers, mainly at the Research Station for Floriculture in Aalsmeer. Favourable results, to the extent of a 35% increase in flower yield, were achieved with *Anthurium andreanum* (Oil-cloth Flower). Research finished only when the greenhouses where the experiments were carried out had to be demolished.

Water culture as a means of growing vegetables

Because water culture makes it possible to control plant nutrition fully, T.N.O. sponsored experiments, initially into the growing of cucumbers and tomatoes, at the research station for fruit and vegetable culture under glass in Naalwijk.

In the case of cucumbers, there was one very good harvest, followed by problems which could not be solved. The cultivation of tomatoes in water did not appear to go down well with growers. It became

An example of plants grown under Hydroculture — tightly packed yet all doing well.

20

These giant Dracaenas *growing to about 12 feet illustrate the full potential of Hydroculture and show that experimentation has been going on for a good many years.*

21

apparent, however, that water and earth demanded different varieties of plant. The best results in water culture were obtained with types that are only moderately successful in earth, including the varieties specifically bred for fast formation of fruit. From experiments carried out by growers, the Agricultural Economy Institute concluded that soilless cultivation is financially justifiable in the Netherlands, at least when carried out in a big way, in spite of higher investment costs.

The early bad publicity that arose from putting water culture into practice before enough of the problems had been sorted out detracted as much as the high initial costs from its acceptance. Besides this, there is little necessity for hydroculture when reasonably good soil is still readily available for vegetable growing.

From experiment to commercial hydroculture

In Germany and particularly Switzerland, plant lovers were growing indoor plants in water experimentally 25 years ago. One of them was Gerard Baumann from Bümplitz near Berne. The seed firm, Vätter, established in Berne, sold everything agricultural from mowers to cattle fodder as well as troughs, basalt silt, gravel and food tablets. Baumann was conveniently placed for advice on hydroculture, because Vätter were among the most important pioneers, and had in his home one of the first experimental hydroculture troughs. His research continued to expand. Having no doubt examined the older methods of water culture and become aware of the advantages and disadvantages, he developed completely new ideas about the technical equipment needed for growing indoor plants in water. When he was satisfied with his results, Baumann submitted his plans to Vätter and about 15 years ago, in close cooperation, formed Luwasa-Interhydro A.G.

After careful preparation, Futz Enche, director of the Frankfurt Palmengarten, set up an exhibition promoted by Luwasa in Germany in the summer of 1965. It was then possible to make use of the long years of experience by establishing Luwasa branches in other countries. There, too, plant lovers, florists and nurserymen had not been idle. Experiments on the growing of indoor plants in water were already under way.

Hydroculture for amateur growers

As we have seen, much of the research into hydroculture over the last few decades has concentrated on the growing of nursery crops like tomatoes and cucumbers. The question was how to put the experience acquired to use with indoor plants. The method of growing apparently had many advantages and, of course, one great disadvantage.

Let us start with the snags: apart from the need for accessories like water level meters, a plant grown under hydroculture is more expensive than one grown in earth, for there is a clear difference between the types of root system. You cannot with impunity take a plant out of a pot of earth, rinse the soil from the roots and expect the plant to go straight on growing in water. If the plants have not grown in water from the start, the ground roots have to be broken down biologically and replaced by the plant with a modified root system, all of which requires care and special treatment. Firms setting out to specialize in hydroculture therefore need to invest in fairly expensive equipment, which for the time being raises the cost of an established plant.

The care of plants afterwards is minimal, which many people consider an advantage. Others, whose urge may be to bring Nature more intimately into their surroundings, might be put off by the feeling that plants which no longer rely on earth for life will no longer need their owners' cosseting. They may be deterred by the mistaken view that the care they give their plants will have to be replaced by a knowledge of chemistry and plant nutrition. In fact, few amateur growers need a high level of technical knowledge to derive pleasure from hydroculture, though the information is available for them if they want to seek it.

On the credit side, plants have a better chance of thriving under hydroculture. The earth in a pot often stops containing any nutrients after about a year; it can be soured by over watering and the presence of bacteria, and it may contain harmful insects. Repotting, when necessary for these or other reasons, is a disturbance which almost inevitably hinders growth, though it is not hard work in the home,

A cross-section of a trough showing the granules it contains and the adapted roots.

for skilful plant lovers will do it themselves, even looking on it as a form of relaxation.

Since you provide in hydroculture a growing medium which has the properties of top-quality soil, containing all the nutrients plants require without contamination by harmful bacteria, pests or toxic substances, you do not have to worry about the state of the earth. Aeration is a very easy matter with the coarser types of growing medium, which inevitably enclose air spaces where the roots can find the oxygen they need. This makes hydroculture a very practicable activity for disabled gardeners, even out of doors, where growing troughs can be placed at a convenient height and there is no need to rely on anyone else for digging and the other heavy tasks of cultivation.

In the absence of food deficiencies and specific diseases, the same species can be grown time and time again without any of the breaks for rotation needed with earth-grown crops. If diseases do come in from external sources, the growing medium can generally be cleaned. The introduction of air-borne weeds is easy to control.

Consistently favourable conditions bring the further benefits of clean crops or matched blooms, which can be produced regularly often in a higher yield—all of which is of special importance to commercial growers. The efficient use of water and nutrients is even more valuable in areas of the world where demand for fresh crops normally exceeds supply through infertility of the soil or scarcity of water.

Plants potted in earth have to be provided with water as they need it; for some plants in sunny positions this will be every day. What happens when everybody is busy?—the plant is given an uncontrolled quantity of water regardless of its needs. And what about the watering if you go away on holiday for a few weeks?

With hydroculture, the plant is watered to the upper limit of the water level meter every two to four weeks. You cannot give too little or too much. The plant regulates its own food and water intake, always using the correct amount. In fact, it is essential to allow the plant time between waterings; the water level must be allowed to drop, so that oxygen can reach the roots. How many indoor plants are ruined because the earth around them is too dry for days on end and then receives a soaking that cuts off the oxygen supply? Even the amount of water available to the plant becomes less in these circumstances, as the earth packs together. As well as the benefit to the plant's development of an even supply of food and water, less frequent watering means less work, which can be important in hospitals, hotels and factories, where time and effort are at a premium.

So, which plants can be grown under hydroculture? In principle, all of them. Even cacti—in most instances these desert plants respond to hydroculture very well. Commercial growers can raise all their normal crops under hydroculture, and amateurs can grow anything they like from indoor pot plants to vegetable crops in versions of commercial beds which are as large as their available space allows. Since competition between plants for nutrients is removed, plants can be packed as closely as is possible without depriving any of them of light.

*An
experimental
form of
Hydroculture!*

Methods of hydroculture

All methods of hydroculture depend on the provision of food together with water to plants, which are given some means of support.

In the method associated with Dr Gericke (the true 'hydroponics'), the roots are bathed with water and nutrient solution, while support is provided above the water container. Alternatively, the plants can grow with their roots in a substratum (sand, vermiculite or leca granules, for example) much as they would in earth, the difference being that the growing medium itself makes no contribution to feeding, which is provided in solution with the water. In either case, the nutrient solution can be made available to the roots in as simple or as sophisticated a manner as you find convenient.

Individual plants can be grown in a simple version of the first method, using a wide-necked jar or other vessel. First find a cork that fits the top of your container, make a hole through the centre, and cut the cork in half so that it can be fitted together around the plant stem.

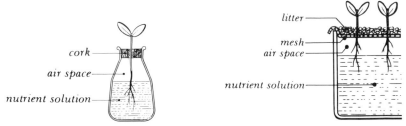

Pad the hole with cotton wool or tissue. Fill the jar with water and nutrients, leaving space at the top. As roots need to be in darkness, cover the sides of glass or clear plastic jars with paper. Aeration of the nutrient mixture can be provided by shaking the jar hard after removing the plant; this should be done every three days or so.

Hydroculture brings a natural atmosphere to offices.

For more plants, any wide container can be used. It will need a rigid lid of wire mesh, covered with a layer of wood wool (white, the red type is harmful), shavings, sawdust, straw, peat moss, a mixture of vermiculite and peat, or some other litter to exclude light from the root space. The nutrient solution still has to be aerated. You can stir it instead of shaking (as with the jar), or bale some of it out and replace it.

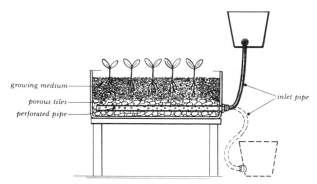

Pots using the same principle, sold as complete sets, have a jar to hold the solution covered with a wire mesh tray holding stone chips to support the plant, and a lid through which the plant stem passes. Developed in Switzerland, these containers are sold in several sizes under the name of Plantanova.

An uncompromisingly modern trough makes its own decorative statement, whilst the plant that it houses ensures a leafy natural atmosphere.

When the plants are grown with their roots in the substratum, they need a container with drainage, like a plant pot or a wooden box lined with polythene and drilled with drainage holes low in the sides. In the bottom of the container, there should be a layer of pebbles or broken crocks, as in soil cultivation. It is very important to make sure that whatever you use in the container is perfectly clean, so wash the drainage material and the growing medium carefully in clear water. When the drainage layer is in place, fill the pot with sand, vermiculite, or whatever growing medium you have chosen, to within about ½ in. (12.54 mm.) of the container's rim. Then you can plant your seeds, seedlings or cuttings. All you need do afterwards is pour on water and nutrient solution mixed, or water in dry nutrient powder, daily in hot, dry weather and less frequently in cool conditions.

Keep the growing medium moist, while ensuring that adequate aeration is taking place. Provide an outer container in which the excess water and nutrient solution can collect and be re-absorbed to replace liquid lost by evaporation. Once a week, flush the substratum with clear water and allow it to drain.

For a large container holding a lot of plants, it is really better to use some means of sub-irrigation, letting in water and nutrient solution at the base, so that the container is evenly and regularly fed. A simple method is to connect the inlet to a flexible pipe (such as a length of hose) running from a reservoir tank (a bucket is convenient) which can be lifted daily to allow the water and food solution to run into the tank and allowed to rest below the level of the plant trough between times for drainage.

You will naturally need to protect the inlet from blockage by particles of the growing medium, which may be done by connecting another piece of hose, with perforations made along it, to the inlet inside the trough and either coiling it underneath a sheet of glass or thin, rigid plastic, or running it across the bottom of the trough through a line of porous, semi-cylindrical tiles (if space allows). Another possibility is to fix a piece of plastic mesh or gauze across the inside of the inlet opening. This is not necessary, of course, if you stand the plants in pots in the tank.

Some means (a hook, or a conveniently placed shelf) will be needed to hold the reservoir bucket when it is raised, and the size of this type of arrangement is of necessity limited by the volume of water which can be lifted. For adequate irrigation, the bucket should be able to hold about 50% of the volume of the tank. A five-gallon bucket, full, weighs about 50 lbs. Allowing enough depth in the tank for root development (e.g. about 8 in. for tomatoes), two gallons will provide irrigation for about one square foot. There is no such limitation to the reservoir tank size if you are prepared to construct a system using pumps. However you manage the irrigation, the principle is to flood and then drain the trough, so that the water and nutrient solution displace old, stale air which may be replaced by fresh air drawn in as the fluid drains away.

You will be able to work out other systems to suit yourself; there are many. In some, water and nutrient solution rise by capillary action, either through a layer of sand or fine aggregate to plants standing in pots, or by a wick which runs from the base of the pot to a reservoir of water below. Others depending on flat, absorbent mats moistened with water and nutrient solution are good for sprouting seeds in the same way as large-scale grass growing units providing animal fodder.

A new method (nutrient film technique) has been welcomed by commercial growers, notably for the cultivation of tomatoes. Plants are held in position by a plastic tube which almost encloses them and is loosely fastened around the stems; food solution which is also rich in oxygen trickles through the tubes, simply bathing the roots or moistening a substratum of paper fibre or Rockwool.

Cuttings in brown clay granules.

Less frequent watering

Hydroculture on a large scale demands technical adaptation by commercial growers, and the expense of the initial investment still means that there are fewer established plants grown under hydro-culture than we may hope to see on the market.

For this reason, plant troughs for cultivation in earth have been developed, mainly in France, with which watering has been reduced to once every two to four weeks. They often take the form of troughs

No guess work! The water level indicator shown here lets you know when the plant needs watering.

equipped with filling tubes and water level meters and enclosing an inner pot which reaches about two-thirds of its inside depth. The bottom of the inner pot is perforated to allow water through and is covered with a synthetic absorbent mat, to which is attached a wick that takes up water and nutrient solution from water contained in the bottom of the outer pot. As soon as a plant is set in the upper part of the pot, the earth needs to be watered until the roots are established. After that, water and eventually food solution are poured through the filling tube into the reservoir. When they have grown through the porous mat, the ground roots reach the water, then becoming water roots. Above the water there is a pocket of air which filters in through a small opening and provides a little space if too much water is added to the reservoir. Filling often results in the spilling of water under the pot, so that some protection for window sill, table or floor covering is advisable.

The main advantage of this system is that there is no need for the cultivation of special plants. Costs are low, since almost all plants are still started off in earth. However, the many snags of earth cultivation remain. If we have to replace plants or change the earth, it is also necessary to renew the synthetic mat. The old one cannot be re-used, as it will have been damaged by the roots.

These water supply systems are sold under a bewildering variety of names. Among them are the still fairly expensive pots fitted with a mirror to show the level of water in the reservoir.

The same system can be made to work without a sythetic mat if the trough is one-third filled with leca granules before adding the earth in which the plants are set. Water is poured into the lower part through the filling tube, and for the first three months (after that only occasionally) also on the surface. If all goes well, the roots grow towards the water and nutrients, taking in what they need.

There are also simplified methods of watering, even with normal clay pots, to allow the plant to control its own intake—which is definitely to be preferred to uncontrolled watering. The principle often depends on a wick that enters the earth by way of the hole in the base of the plant pot and is in contact with absorbent foam material in the bottom of an ornamental outer container or with water in a special dish which acts as a reservoir. The plant can obtain water in this way for about two weeks, after which the reservoir must be filled, or the foam moistened. These, and other systems, are more or less dependent on earth; however, the common principle is less frequent watering.

The materials replacing earth

Certain properties are required of the growing medium used to support the plants. Its structure has to allow good circulation of air and water. The ideal is for the substratum to absorb water, retain it for a time and release it gradually.

In general, the medium's ability to hold water depends on the size of the particles making it up. Small particles, having a high surface area in relation to their size, are able to hold much water, but are

A close-up of ceramic Hydroculture troughs.

separated by small air spaces. Irregular spaces (gravel chips, say, as opposed to spherical particles) have good water retention, and porous particles, holding more water than impermeable ones of the same size, make it possible to use larger particles with correspondingly larger air spaces between them.

Materials should neither be too fine nor cling together, nor should they break down, which would produce the disadvantages of too fine a texture, interfering with good drainage and preventing oxygen from reaching the roots, with the added danger of sharp edges which may damage roots. A good substratum has, too, to be chemically harmless; it must not contain substances which could change the composition of the food solution.

Many of the media tried in research over the years are still in use. They include sand, which is fairly easy to obtain. It should not be made up of grains that are too fine or uneven in size (in which case the finer grains may settle in the bottom of the trough, holding on to the water needed by the roots above). If you are not sure of its composition, try growing a few seeds in a small quantity of the sand to test for toxic substances, etc. If they develop into healthy plants, go ahead. Those types sold commercially for horticultural purposes are clean. Any gravel from granite, shale, sandstone, quartzite, ironstone, pumice, and even cinders or broken bricks can be used, though watch out for a tendency for some types to break down into sharp particles.

Other possibilities are perlite, vermiculite and lignite. Vermiculite is a silicate mineral which has been heated until it expands to enclose air cells. It is light, absorbent and sterile; it is a bad conductor of heat and therefore a 'warm' medium for the germination of seeds and a good one for tender young plants. However, long use or constant heavy rainfall can break it down to a waterlogged mass, so that there are drawbacks in using it out of doors, when the light weight also gives it a tendency to blow about in wind. In some places, vermiculite is in short supply.

Perlite, a rock related to granite, is extensively used in America. Also expanded by heat, it is less likely to break down under normal conditions than vermiculite, while possessing many of its advantages. Lignite—brown coal, found in the west of England—is highly absorbent. It is like peat, in that it is an organic material, possessing negligible food value to plants, but it is tougher and takes longer to break down.

When indoor plants are bought, already established, from nurseries, the medium surrounding their roots is often light brown granules, available in England through Rochfords under the name Hydroleca. This material, produced by the expansion of clay particles at a temperature of about 1200° C, embodies many of the qualities required of a growing medium. The granules are inert, reducing the risk of infection, they can absorb as much as a third of their own weight of water, and are small enough to encourage capillary action.

Originally developed in America as a light material for use in the shipping industry, clay which had been baked and expanded into hard crumbs was adopted for use in insulation by the building trade, where it became known as Haydite after the inventor, Dr Hayd. It was 1936 before the material was heard of in Europe, where it was first produced in Denmark. A special oven was developed in 1938, and the granules were called leca (light expanded clay aggregate).

The Leca group, formed in 1964, now has branches in twelve European countries. The granules are distributed in three sizes: 0-3 mm. for cuttings, 3-10 mm. and 10-22 mm. for potting plants and filling troughs. Nowadays, the granules are also used for improvement of earth for cultivation and as substratum in roof gardens. The expensive roof areas, normally unused, can be employed to give room for more open-air recreation, separated completely from traffic.

Roof garden:

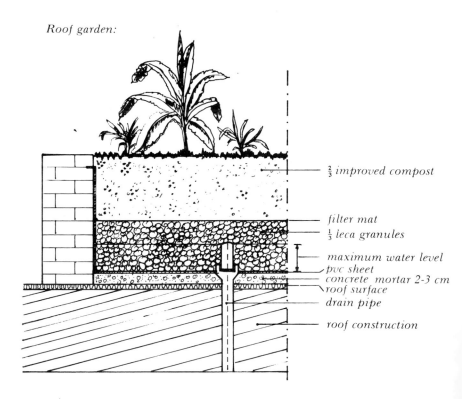

$\frac{2}{3}$ *improved compost*

filter mat
$\frac{1}{3}$ *leca granules*

maximum water level
pvc sheet
concrete mortar 2-3 cm
roof surface
drain pipe

roof construction

Among the synthetic materials used as growing media there are expanded polyurethane flakes, manufactured by Bayer as Baystrat; Styromull or Polystyrol and other, similar materials are made by various firms.

The growing media used for cuttings

Some years ago, cuttings taken in hydroculture were put into: fine pebbles, gravel, plastoil (a synthetic foam) or perlite. The use of certain substrata changes quickly. Lately, we have seen an increase in the use of small blocks of Rockwool, or the kind of gravel that is familiar on tennis courts. The Rockwool used in small blocks is specially treated material expanded so that it can take up a prodigious amount of water—only a very small portion of the volume consists of dry matter, and the water is absorbed very quickly, even when the Rockwool is dry. The material holds no threat to the environment.

The small size of leca granules are often used. Another growing medium, Terragreen, is quite new. It consists of granules of clay from Mississippi, fired at a temperature of 800° C and ranging from 0.6 to 2.5 mm. in size. Terragreen is also used in the topsoil of golf courses and as litter for cat trays.

Of course, there are still other substrata that may be used for cuttings; vermiculite is one. Every nurseryman will achieve the best results with the one he has chosen, in spite of its possible disadvantages.

The intake of water and food solution

The processes involved when a plant grows and flowers are very complex. One of them is the intake of water and nourishment through the roots. The energy needed for this is produced from sugars, which have been formed in the leaves, and oxygen.

For most plant roots, the oxygen must be available in the water around them. Normally moist earth contains a certain quantity of water, but 20-30% of its volume is composed of air spaces from which the oxygen dissolved in the soil water is replenished. It is logical, then, that a plant in earth which is continually soaked grows badly, for the necessary oxygen is displaced by water, which lingers around the roots and encourages the soil particles to cling together. When a

If there were any fears that the modern hydroculture trough had its limitations in terms of surroundings this picture should dispel them for you.

Plants have the capacity to choose the foods they need — grass takes in a high quantity of silicon.

non-absorbent substratum like gravel is used, the plants stand dry and are thus able to obtain oxygen, but must be watered regularly and, at times, very often. However, leca granules, as has been mentioned before, and some other substrata are particularly absorbent.

Briefly, to encourage our plants to grow, we must supply them with water and nutrients which they can absorb by a process requiring oxygen. It is also important to recognize that plants have a capacity for selection. Hence, grass takes in a lot of silicon (silicic acid), while other plants require only a little. Certain plants may take a lot more of one material from the earth than others.

Plants grown in earth can take in elements from the soil if they are given no other nourishment, but in hydroculture care must be taken to provide all the elements in the right proportion and concentration in the water, or the plant will suffer from deficiencies.

Research into the nutritional requirements of plants has established that they absorb the following chemical substances from the root's surroundings: nitrogen, phosphorus, potassium, calcium, magnesium, sulphur, a smaller quantity of iron and even smaller amounts of the trace elements, which include boron, manganese, copper and zinc. In addition, they need the gases carbon dioxide, hydrogen and oxygen from the water and air.

The form in which the elements are assimilated and their importance to the plant vary considerably. It is therefore essential to use a well-balanced food solution containing all of them. Deficiencies are characterized by certain symptoms: a plant which is obtaining too little nitrogen will display poor growth, and its leaves will have a pale or yellowish look; a lack of phosphorus results in

39

dull looking, dark leaves, sometimes blemished with patches of discoloration; potassium deficiency shows in mottled and, later, scorched looking leaves, but is not always easy to spot; calcium deficiency produces stunted growth and dark green, wrinkled leaves; in cases of magnesium deficiency the older leaves are often patchy in colour; and in sulphur deficiency yellowing leaves often have patches of discoloration at the base. A lack of available iron will result in yellow, scorched looking leaves. It should be remembered that, since plants have a limited range of signs by which they can show us that something is wrong, symptoms may have a number of meanings. Yellowed leaves, as well as appearing in cases of mineral deficiency, can also indicate a lack of air round the roots, which can be rectified by regular and, for a time, more frequent aeration of the roots. It may, too, be the result of overcrowding of the roots, which necessitates repotting, or other conditions, such as unsuitable temperature or the presence of fumes in the surrounding atmosphere.

Excesses of nutrients are harmful, too. The growing medium may become mouldy, the plant grows abnormally, older plants suffer from browning at the leaf edges, roots die off, and the water develops an unpleasant smell. Even if we discover the mistake in time, the best we can do is to rinse the plant, cut off affected roots and repot in fresh substratum. Trouble is better prevented by taking care to give the right dose of nutrient solution.

In order to experience the greatest lasting pleasure from plants in hydroculture, it is wise to use a special mixed fertilizer. Though plants grown in earth will be satisfied with a solution intended for hydroculture, the reverse is not the case. The combination for plants in earth is generally not appropriate in hydroculture, and certain elements will be missing.

There are already different makes of mixed fertilizers available in powder, tablet and liquid form. Suppliers of hydroculture equipment or established plants will usually provide or recommend nutrients which their experience and research have shown to be suitable (Barclic Products offer Libsol and Phostrogen; Rochfords sell Lewatit HD 5). It is not really a good idea to try mixing your own nutrients; many of the elements are costly in the small quantities that will be required, and they are not always readily available to the amateur. Very careful measurement of small quantities is not an easy matter. The manufacturers provide reliable mixtures from standard nutrient formulae. Phostrogen is a good example, easily obtainable from many stockists in Britain, or from the manufacturers for other countries. You must, and this is important, read the instructions on the package before using any nutrient mixture. Never increase the

Soluble mixed fertilizers in different forms — liquid and (front) feeding capsules.

prescribed concentration, and adjust its strength according to the manufacturer's recommendations—a weaker concentration is often necessary for seedlings or cuttings, while mature plants will require the normal strength. Weaker solutions are sometimes advisable in hot weather, when much water will be lost by evaporation. Follow the instructions on how often the nutrients should be given.

The formulae which are based on standard nutrient salts should be flooded out of troughs with clean water at the interval suggested by the manufacturer to protect the balance of the solution, which could be upset by a build up of unused salts. When the container has been drained, feeding should be carried on as normal.

Nutrients are applied, as we have seen, with the water that is given to the plants. In simple systems, the water and nutrient solution can be sprinkled on the surface of the growing medium with a fine rose on the watering can. Nutrients supplied in powder form will have to be mixed with the water first, of course. It is usually recommended that the solution, when mixed, is left overnight, to allow time for the slower substances to dissolve. If you make up a quantity of solution and wish to store some of it, keep it in the dark, as light conditions can slowly reduce the available iron contained in the solution. When pouring on the liquid, you should aim to make the medium suitably moist, not soaking. How often to irrigate depends on a number of factors which affect the rate of evaporation: the humidity and temperature of the surrounding air, the amount of wind, the position of the container and so on. Experience is your best guide; in practice, the need is usually daily in summer and less often in cool weather. Some of the growing media, like vermiculite, are more capable of holding water than others, and this also helps to determine the frequency of irrigation.

Overhead watering is wasteful of nutrient solution. With a small plant container, you can collect the excess in a dish or saucer under the pot, so that it can be re-absorbed as evaporation takes place. This also provides a means of leaving the plant to take care of itself for a day or two if you cannot attend to it: simply leave a small reservoir of water and nutrient solution in the saucer.

Fertilizers in powder form can simply be sprinkled on the substratum around single plants or along the rows and then watered in. It is a simple, economical method of cultivation on a small scale, but presents difficulties with low, leafy plants, like lettuce, which may not leave sufficiently large an area of substratum exposed between them. In that case, it would perhaps be better to water on a nutrient solution, such as Maxicrop, which will be absorbed through the foliage. Storage of powders presents no problems.

When systems are based on sub-irrigation, small containers can simply be stood in water and nutrient solution for about half an hour before draining. Larger systems are fed and watered by any of the available means, pumps, valves or siphons.

Some nutrient supplies depend on artificial resins. Often called ion exchange fertilizers, they release nutrient salts into the water continuously in the quantities used by the plant, at the same time absorbing harmful or useless substances from the water. One advantage is that you do not have to empty the trough to remove the unused salts, and another is the elimination of any risk of giving an overdose of nutrients—this makes less frequent application feasible (the usual interval is six months) with only the replacement of water necessary in the meantime (at three to six-week intervals). The Bayer product, Lewatit HD 5 is marketed in England by Rochfords. Note that these nutrients are *not* suitable for use with food plants and that they should be kept out of the reach of children and pets. Some synthetic resins are supplied in small perforated boxes, referred to as feeding patterns, which are simply dropped into the water.

Use tap water with artificial resin fertilizers—rainwater, while it is seldom completely pure in practice, does not contain enough dissolved substances to react with the fertilizer and needs to be treated before use. If very hard water is used, a harmless white deposit may occur on the surface of the substratum.

42

Municipal water is almost always suitable for use in hydroculture. The main defect is likely to be over heavy chlorination, which can be at least partially remedied by allowing the water to stand in a wide-topped container overnight and giving it the occasional stir. If you are in any doubt about the composition of your tap water, your local council or water board will probably be willing to provide you with an analysis. One of the factors mentioned is likely to be the pH level (a measure of acidity and alkalinity). Most water supplies will mix with the nutrients you use to give a pH value which is near 6.0 and thus suitable for nearly all plants. However, the plants' intake of nutrients may cause changes in the level, so that it is worth checking periodically, especially a week or two after setting up a new trough or giving a complete change of water and nutrient solution. A Universal Indicator solution (an example is manufactured by British Drug Houses) should be used. The mixture changes colour when added, as directed, to a sample of the nutrient solution, enabling you to read off the pH value from a printed colour chart. Indicator papers, which also change colour, are available.

Taking hydroculture to the office is an obvious move. Even if your secretary doesn't know a Crossandra from a Rhipsalis, looking after plants grown under hydroculture is child's play.

How to cultivate your own plant in water

The easiest and most satisfactory way to grow plants in water is to start with a cutting taken by any of the appropriate methods. Pelargoniums (*Geranium*) and Fuchsias are among those which can be propagated from a top shoot, African Violets (*Saintpaulia*) will grow from the stem of a detached leaf, and still other plants from a section of stem with one leaf attached.

It is better to propagate plants in water than to attempt to transfer established plants to water from earth, since any disturbance may hinder growth and should, for that reason, be avoided. In practice, commercial growers try to cultivate as many plants as possible from cuttings, but as long as demand exceeds supply in hydroculture, especially for large specimens of such types as *Ficus*, *Monstera* and other popular plants, they will be forced to change many plants from earth to water.

Plant lovers know that the top and side shoots which make the best cuttings have to be at the right stage of growth, not too young nor too old, and not in flower. The condition of the shoot is very important in hydroculture, and of course the plant must be free from disease.

The twig should be cut with a sharp knife immediately below a joint or growth bud to a length of 2-4 in. (5-10 cm.), with a few exceptions. In general, there should be three to five single leaves, or two to three pairs, not counting the top shoot. The wound will soon heal with new tissue that, in turn, produces roots. It is important to know that broken shoots have greater difficulty in producing cork. Cuttings from juicy plants, like geraniums, must be left for a few hours after removal from the plant to allow the cut surface to dry. Those from harder plants may even take some days, and the wounds of plants containing latex, such as the species of *Euphorbia* (*horrida*, *pulcherrima*) and some cacti must be briefly burned, so that the shoot does not 'bleed to death'.

The cuttings can now stand in a bottle containing a little water, in as light a position as possible to prevent rotting, but not in full, drying sunlight. The water should not be too deep, especially to begin with; the level can be increased later, step by step. The shoot

Cuttings in a bottle of water, and small blocks of Rockwool.

can be prevented from drying out by enclosing it in an indoor propagator or plastic bag. The cuttings must, as far as possible, be separated from each other (i.e. not touching).

Of course, the container does not have to be a bottle. Anything that is practicable may be used, for instance glass troughs or plastic pots. When support is needed to hold the shoot upright, use a net or wire mesh stretched over the pot or trough.

Pots for hydroculture are available from specialist seedsmen, florists and garden centres. Slow-growing plants, like Cacti, certainly benefit from the use of special pots in which they can be left in peace. Like other plants, they prefer a warm base, particularly in their early development, and should not be placed on a cold floor. In any event, a temperature of at least 20° C must be maintained to ensure quick root formation, but it must not exceed 26° C.

When growing cuttings in individual pots or a glass trough, we can make use of a substratum instead of the mesh for their support. It is important for the shoots, especially the smaller ones, to be set in fine-grained material, like sand or vermiculite, which readily takes up water. Specialist hydroculturalists use leca granules (the smallest size), fine gravel, Terragreen, or Rockwool. The cuttings, planted dry in the substratum, are dampened only by a mist from a spray. They should neither be allowed to dry out completely nor become waterlogged.

At the outset, and this goes for all cuttings, food solution is added to the water in pot or substratum only in very weak concentration. For many plants, it is even better not to add any nourishment at all in the beginning. By the time the cuttings are well advanced, the food is given in greater concentration, according to the manufacturer's recommendations.

Some of the plants which root easily in earth (*Cissus*, for example) have conspicuous difficulty in establishing themselves in water. The opposite is true in the case of *Fittonia*, which roots very easily even when a cutting is simply stood in a glass of water.

Any of the other propagation techniques can be carried out in hydroculture without difficulty. Layered stems, runners and aerial roots, as well as rhizomes, tubers and bulbs will become established in beds of warm, absorbent material like vermiculite.

Sowing seeds in water

Until now, we have been considering vegetative reproduction, by means of shoots. The rooting of seeds is equally possible. Terragreen, perlite and vermiculite are among suitable media for germination.

To plant seeds: using a fine rose on the watering can, soak the sand, vermiculite or other substratum until water runs from the drainage holes in the seed tray. With your finger or a pointed stick, make grooves along the surface to the depth at which you would normally plant the particular type of seed (this is usually mentioned on the packet), drop the seeds in place and sprinkle the surface with water, taking care not to press the substratum down. Tiny seeds can simply be scattered evenly over the surface, then sprinkled with dry growing material and afterwards watered.

It is important to start the seeds off in a warm, moist atmosphere which can be provided in indoor propagators, whether heated or not, or simply by a sheet of glass or clear plastic. Special containers for growing seeds under hydroculture are available in Germany and Switzerland, but with the use of a little imagination they are not really necessary for germination. Plastic seed trays, or shallow wooden fruit boxes with perforated polythene linings are fine.

When the seed or cutting has grown into a plant with good water roots, it can be transferred to a pot or trough filled with leca granules (3-20 mm.). If you are transplanting seedlings from soil, vermiculite or sand to another medium, uproot the seedlings with a spoon, wash off soil or, in the case of vermiculite or sand, shake off excess, place the whole root system in a hole in the new medium, replace the material round the seedling and firm it in; all this should be done very gently. Allow the same space that you would give the seedlings if they were to be grown on in soil, and plant them deeply enough for their entire roots to be in water during irrigation of the container. Always soak the substratum before transplanting—seedlings can be removed more easily if the medium is wet, and they need to be transferred to one that is well watered. Afterwards, however, watering should be sparing—too much discourages root development. It is sometimes a good idea not to add nutrients for a day or two.

Planting in water / washing

The increasing demand for well-developed plants established under hydroculture makes it necessary, for the present, to convert into water growers, plants which were originally planted in earth. Although this is not easy, it can be done indoors. The plants must be strong, healthy, not too old (about two years), and preferably not a flowering type or one with a delicate root structure. Spring and summer are the most favourable times.

After tapping the plant out of the pot, roll the root ball between the hands to remove the earth from the roots. Then rinse the root system clean in a bucket of tepid water until all the earth is removed. The plant may then be potted with well soaked and perfectly clean substratum in a container with slits in the sides. This can be a conical pot of synthetic material. Pots made of expanded polystyrene are also used, but this material wears less well and is sometimes pierced by the roots, as also happens in the case of Odoul baskets (black plastic baskets, like pot-sized strainers, for use instead of the normal inner pots). The basket is useful nevertheless in allowing the necessary oxygen easy access to the roots.

After potting, the plant is then stood in a trough with water, again not too cold, reaching a third of the way up the pot. It is sensible to change the water regularly so that fresh oxygen reaches the roots each time. The ground roots are gradually broken down by a biological process requiring oxygen, and new water roots are formed.

Water roots differ from ground roots both externally and internally, and some of the characteristics are clear to the naked eye. The roots which grow in earth are often strong, thick and much branched; the root hairs are short and relatively sturdy. The roots of a plant grown in hydroculture are less strong, less branched, and have long, delicate root hairs. It is evident from their construction that ground roots meet with a lot more resistance than those grown in water.

During the process of changing over, the plants need to be in good light, preferably not direct sunlight, and a damp atmosphere. Suitable plants generally survive the upheaval reasonably well, though some leaves may turn yellow and drop, and the occasional plant will die. Indeed, transferring a plant to hydroculture is a very good way of improving unsatisfactory growth.

Preparing an earthborn plant for a hydroculture trough.

The plant's root and earth support system are tapped out of the pot.

Earth is rolled out of the roots.

The roots are further cleaned in water.

The brown granules that will now support the plant must be rinsed in water.

A suitable pot must be selected.

The cleaned plant is re-potted in granules.

The plant stands in water — to $\frac{1}{3}$ pot depth.

The ground roots will be broken down by a biological process that requires oxygen.

The odoul basket with its many air holes provides plenty of oxygen but does not constrict the roots.

Look at the way the roots have forced their way out of this expanded polystyrene container.

A cross section showing the roots of a plant re-potted from soil. Note that they are firm with short root hairs.

These roots support a plant grown under Hydroculture. Note that they are soft and supple with long fine root hairs.

51

An example of a healthy
Yucca aloifolia *grown*
under Hydroculture.

Under nursery conditions the plants are washed, potted and placed in large communal troughs.

It is possible to increase the oxygen content by growing the plants in a trough designed to accommodate running water.

An example of potted plants growing in a large still-water trough. Under these conditions a nutrient solution will be added as necessary.

Good conditions

Though conditions in the greenhouse of commercial hydroculture specialists have been carefully thought out with a view to making the development of water roots as trouble free as possible, we meet wide variations in· their treatment of the plants after rinsing. The nurseryman places washed plants in large, rectangular waterproof troughs, often made of concrete. These cultivating troughs are filled with water, generally at the temperature prevailing in the greenhouse. Some growers add food solution to the water immediately, others much later; the constituents of the mixture, and its strength, frequently vary.

Some nurseries increase the amount of oxygen available by supplying the roots with running water, which is pumped in at one end and drains through the sloping trough to a pipe at the other end which returns it to a reservoir tank. This method of automatic irrigation provides a change of oxygen both by displacing the air held in the spaces between the particles of the growing medium, allowing fresh air to be drawn in when drainage occurs, and because each new supply of water has been freshly oxygenated. A further refinement is the pumping of additional oxygen into the slowly running water. These measures are intended to achieve the root change as quickly as possible, for time is money. The time allowed for developing water roots varies among growers from about two to about ten weeks, depending upon the kind of plant. Of course there are failures: as many as 5% of the plants may fail to survive—large Yuccas and some tall varieties of Ficus are among the most vulnerable. Nurserymen, with an eye on their profits, naturally try to keep the failure rate as low as possible.

While there are variations in the temperature of the water used in the growing troughs, it is best in all cases for it not to be too cold. The plants generally stand in water alone (nutrient solution is sometimes added), but the occasional nursery will surround the plant pots with leca granules or gravel in the troughs.

When the ground roots have broken down and been replaced by established water roots, the plants still have to become used to an indoor environment for later sale or use in propagation. Again, there are different methods of achieving this hardening off. When seedlings are grown in outdoor units, removal of the shelter increases the passage of water out through the leaves and helps to prevent wilting. Some growers dry their plants out once in a while, removing the water from the troughs to allow extra oxygen to reach the roots. The varied methods used by specialist growers to achieve a good end product, in this case a plant under hydroculture, can be imitated at home to encourage the plants to thrive.

Troughs for indoor plants

The carefully raised cutting or the plant with washed roots stands in a special hydroculture pot. Of course, we can take a plate or a simple dish, place the pot in it and ensure that the level of water and food solution is maintained at about a third of the height of the pot. But a ceramic trough, a glazed stoneware pot, or a glass battery container are preferable in many cases and, naturally, better suited to the indoor environment.

Plants and their containers are increasingly bought as decorative features in circumstances when a cupboard or lampshade might have been considered in the past. It is important, when you are choosing a plant container, to give some thought to how it will fit in with the surroundings. A plant in a brightly coloured synthetic trough does not go with antique furniture, whereas an attractive stoneware container would blend in very well. Troughs of all kinds are suitable for planting as long as they are watertight. This is very important and can save a lot of trouble. It is also essential to ensure that the trough does not stand directly on the floor, or as sometimes happens the floor covering under it may become mouldy through lack of air. The problem can be solved by raising the trough on a few small blocks to ensure free circulation of air underneath. Most manufacturers take care to provide ridges under troughs for this reason.

It is a must, especially with troughs made of synthetic material, to check whether the base has been inserted or made as a whole with the sides, e.g. by extrusion or casting. It sometimes happens that the joint of a welded base loosens under the weight of the contents, resulting in a leaking trough.

Plastic troughs are very durable and come in all imaginable shapes and colours. Large examples are often provided with wheels, and some have a drainage tap. The manufacturers even go so far as to coordinate troughs with furniture and other useful articles. Serviceable utensils made of plastic, modern in form and colour, provide just the right setting for a plant grown under hydroculture.

Also very decorative are troughs and bowls made of plexiglass. The possibilities of these 'panorama' containers are unlimited, because

Plastic troughs are very durable and water-proof. They come in a variety of shapes and sizes

Large troughs are often fitted with wheels to make their moving easier.

Some manufacturers combine troughs with furniture as a complete unit.

A very attractive Hydroculture arrangement in a large container made of Plexiglas.

Transparent troughs make very versatile containers but they are prone to algae.

Some examples of ornamental ceramic pots.

they can be stacked, stood singly and hung up, with or without the domed top, which is so designed as to prevent condensation. Such transparent troughs, however, have the disadvantage of encouraging algal growth. The greenish algae develop in the presence of light in a growing medium which is kept too wet or badly drained and consume nutrients at the expense of the plant. In larger troughs, the growth of algae can be prevented by the use of a waterproof inner trough, with the space between the troughs filled with leca granules or attractively coloured gravel. With troughs that are too small to hold an inner container, it is difficult to discourage the growth of algae. The only sure method of control is to remove the planting from light, which is of course detrimental to the plant. However, with plants that have become sturdy enough, the surface of the substratum can be covered with a layer of stones; algaecides are available if necessary.

Because they are not translucent, asbestos troughs do not suffer from the problem of algae. They are sold in many sizes and shapes, and the outside may be painted. As the material is porous, inner surfaces need to be sealed with a watertight coating. Fibreglass makes a good, durable lining; make sure that any sealer you use is not toxic to plants. Ceramic ornaments, too, need to be treated with a sealing agent unless they are glazed or have been fired at a high temperature (approximately 1300° C). Since much good stoneware is hand made, it

The water level meters indicate the need for attention.

Troughs fitted with their own water level meters.

is often possible to commission a required shape or size. Glazes, compounded and applied as they are by the potter, come in a wide variety of colours and shades, while naturally coloured stoneware is very versatile and suits most interiors in homes and offices. Its aesthetic values are independent of sudden fashion changes, it holds its economic value, and the quiet shades do not compete for attention.

Metal troughs are not often used in hydroculture. An inner trough is essential because oxidation of the metal caused by direct contact with water is very harmful to plants. Synthetic or asbestos cement inner containers are among the most convenient because they are supplied inexpensively in many shapes and sizes. Home made troughs, built with wood or bricks, have to be provided with waterproof inner containers. It is sensible to find out what is available in the way of lining troughs before starting out on your own designs.

Special containers for an individual plant often have a built-in water level meter and consist of separate upper and lower pieces. Other models are provided with special inner containers with side slits.

Equipment for a hydroculture trough

A plant growing in an attractive trough is not always the full story. Accessories can be obtained which are unknown in the cultivation of plants in earth. One is a water level meter, of which there are many types and variations in use. Usually, they consist of a plastic tube, a little longer than the height of the plant pot, with slits cut in the base to allow the passage of water. The tube is topped with clear glass or plastic that eventually protrudes from the substratum and is marked with maximum and minimum water levels; a plastic float is enclosed in the tube to indicate the level of the water. The highest level should be shown when the pot is standing in water up to a third of its height; the minimum level of water is a few centimetres below the bottom of

A selection of water level meters.

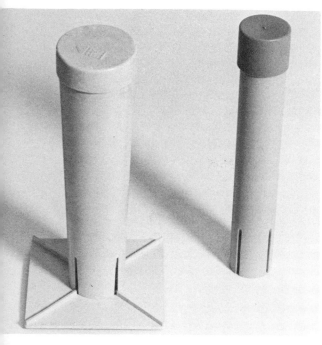

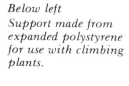

Two different types of
filling tube for topping
up water in a trough.

Below left
Support made from
expanded polystyrene
for use with climbing
plants.

Examples of combined
water level meter and
filling tube.

the pot. It is important to let the level reach minimum before adding more water—otherwise the roots will not be aerated properly.

The water in the trough has to be topped up every two to four weeks by means of the filling tube, which extends to the bottom of the trough. Take care to pour as little water as possible over the substratum, or the roots will find it too easily. They develop better if they have to work to find water. The filling tube may be in plastic with a diameter of a few centimetres appropriate to the size of trough. Of course, there are slits in the base of the tube to let water into the trough, and the top is closed with a stopper. Only in small or crowded troughs can the filling tube be omitted. In such cases, the water and nutrient solution should be poured on the substratum at the side of the trough.

Hydroculture firms often sell pots with combined meters and filling tubes, which are well made in brown or grey plastic. These are convenient in confined spaces. Instructions for their use and maintenance are always supplied with pots that contain them. It is sometimes recommended that you stand the filling tube on a matchstick in the trough in order to provide enough clearance for the dispersal of ion exchange fertilizers when they are poured in.

Supports made of expanded polystyrene are available for use with climbing plants, replacing a branch or stick placed in the trough. Wooden supports, which would in any case rot because of the constant contact with water, are rather old fashioned, but the polystyrene supports can be covered with moss to achieve a much more up to date effect.

Filling an indoor trough

With all the necessities either bought or made, you can now fill a trough.

First, stand the filling tube, of approximately the same height as the trough, on the bottom of the empty trough. For convenience, it should be as close to the edge as possible. After that put in a layer of well-washed leca granules or other chosen growing medium to a level of about 9 in. (20 cm.) from the rim of the trough (the special hydroculture pots are generally just below this in height). The water level meter is placed on top of the granules so that the glass extends above the rim of the trough.

The plants can then be arranged in the trough with their pots reaching just below the level of its rim. Removal of the plants from their individual pots before placing them in an arrangement is not recommended, as the movement of the substratum may cause root damage. The pot keeps substratum and roots together, facilitating

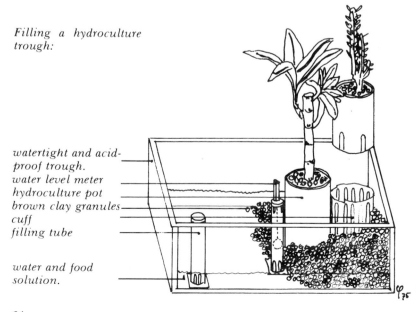

Filling a hydroculture trough:

watertight and acid-proof trough.
water level meter
hydroculture pot
brown clay granules
cuff
filling tube

water and food solution.

64

Essentials for filling a trough.

Pot lips should rest a little below the rim of the trough.

replacement of the plant, which can be done by simply removing both plant and substratum, leaving the pot in position to receive the new plant and its pot. Outer cuffs placed around the individual pots provide another convenient method of changing over plants in poly-styrene pots—when the first is removed, the cuff stays behind for the new plant, and its pot, to be slipped inside.

As plants grown under hydroculture often depend on smaller root systems than those they would develop in earth, potting on is less frequently necessary and should be carried out only if the pot becomes top heavy, which is really a matter of appearance if its pot is stood firmly in a larger arrangement.

Should you need to repot a single plant, however, first soak and carefully wash the new growing medium. If you are using an ion exchange fertilizer, sprinkle the recommended amount in the bottom of the outer container and cover it with a layer of substratum as suggested above, seeing that the bottom of the water level meter is at the same level as the bottom of the inner pot. If it is clear to you that the root system really needs a larger pot, you can select one in a size that is slightly larger, potting the plant on in the growing medium as you would in earth. Some kinds of substratum are easier than others

A natural looking arrangement with plant trailing over the edge of its trough.

Natural stones can be used with great effect when making up an arrangement.

to handle, but even the lightest materials can be scooped with a small flower pot or plastic cup if they have been thoroughly soaked with clean water. Then place the inner pot in the trough, surround it with more of the chosen growing medium and top up with water to the maximum level. If, after a few days, the material seems to have settled unevenly, add enough extra to level it up.

In arranging a number of plants, we have to be careful that the plants will continue to have room to develop attractively. Taller plants should stand at the back of the arrangement. Trailing plants at the edges will eventually grow to hide the filling tube and water meter. When the plants are satisfactorily arranged, the next step is to fill the space between them with leca granules or other coarse growing medium to the level of the trough's rim, hiding the tops of the pots and leaving only the stopper of the filling tube and the glass top of the meter protruding. The trough can then be made more attractive with the addition of pebbles or lumps of lavastone. Anything that is good to look at is fine, as long as it is durable, chemically harmless and inert. Many natural stones are suitable for use in the 'garden'—gravel from rivers, granite, lavasplit, and the bigger grades, such as marble chips and pebbles. A collection of stones picked up on holiday can add a personal touch.

Arrangements

Plant troughs are often filled with an assortment of plants. These 'cocktails' have a lot of disadvantages, apart from their frequently messy appearance. Some plants, especially variegated types, need a lot of light, while others may have different requirements; some may grow fast at the expense of smaller, slower-growing varieties.

Mixed troughs filled with earth have the added problem of varying water needs. *Anthurium andreanum* with high water requirements may be placed with *Cryptanthus* or *Sansevieria* which need less. This is not a difficulty in hydroculture, because all plants then take only enough water for their needs.

One variety per trough grouped for effect.

Mixed plant arrangement — all having the same water requirements.

Over the last few years, however, plant arrangers have been increasingly restricting themselves to one kind of plant per trough. This can be explained by the fact that decorative plants such as Yuccas, long-stemmed Dracaenas, Cacti and *Cyperus alternifolius* are very much in fashion. These plants are often difficult to combine without loss of their decorative value, but many others which were formerly popular, like ferns, palms, Asparagus Fern and *Pelargonium citrosum* (Lemon-scented Geranium) are also very attractive when potted alone. If there is a large space to be filled, several troughs may be placed together. The heights may be varied by raising one trough on another empty one, as well as by using plants of different habit.

The suitability of plants will often depend on the size and colour of the troughs available. Red Cordylines do not look their best in a bright purple trough, while the atmosphere created by a palm may be enhanced even more if it stands in a warm-toned ceramic trough. The colours predominating in the interior as a whole have as great an effect on the plants as their immediate surroundings.

Even experts often find a balanced plant arrangement difficult to achieve. In any case, it is important to consider the living conditions needed by the plants, not place them too close together, and think about the species' relative chances of survival.

A large scale area of mixed plants under hydroculture brings an air of tranquillity to an office setting.

Systems

After arranging the plants in the trough, pour water through the filling tube with nutrient solution until the gauge shows maximum water level. Refilling is necessary only after two to four weeks when, and not before, the level has dropped to minimum. The water in the trough, pot or dish is almost still. This is referred to as a standing water system. Although the different hydroculture firms describe their own versions of this system in various ways, the principle, standing water, stays the same. It is the easiest method to use.

The automatic irrigation method often used in nurseries is more difficult. There, the water is slowly pumped through the troughs, allowing more oxygen to reach the roots. One can fill a trough on this principle of course, but it is a rather expensive business. Perhaps for this reason it is not often used for purposes that are not commercial, but there are now systems which enable troughs of plants in different rooms throughout a building to be maintained automatically from one place; a basement is often convenient. The systems are supplied under the trade names Florever or Maramatic.

Water circulates through the troughs several times a day, with intervals when the plants are almost dry. Several plastic tanks acting as reservoirs for the water and nutrients are connected by pipes to the troughs. The timing is automatically controlled by clocks, and the only tasks that remain are the correction of growth by pruning, spraying leaves with clear water, removing dead ones and generally tidying up.

The same system can be tried out on a small scale in whatever space you have to spare, with a can or bucket and a pump (one taken from an old washing machine would serve) underneath or next to the trough. The reservoir must be connected to the trough with lengths of piping. Although this system is feasible without a timing device, if you do not include a time switch to start the pump to take care of regular irrigation, you will have to start the pump yourself three to five times a day. It will also be necessary to maintain the level of water and nutrient solution in the reservoir.

Detailed instructions on the setting up of large scale systems are not relevant here, but the principle of alternate flooding with water and nutrients to feed the plants and draining to allow oxygen to reach the roots, stressed earlier normally applies.

Self-contained systems with ready constructed pumping unit that are available for the amateur grower include the equipment developed by Barclic Products Ltd. This essentially consists of a bench with two levels; water and nutrient solution bathe the roots of plants growing in channels on the top, and then return along the lower level to a reservoir from which the mixture is recirculated by a pump.

The water in these troughs is quite still.

A modern trough sitting comfortably in a contemporary room and in harmony with the old tiled floor and wooden beams.

The care and maintenance of plants

Plants living in water do need care just as much as those which are planted in earth.

Every two to four weeks, the trough needs topping up with tepid water. This should happen just as the water meter shows the minimum level. When there is a low level of water, oxygen can reach the roots. Normal tap water contains calcium and magnesium salts that the plants need. However, in areas where the water is too hard it is wise to boil it, when some of the hardening substances will turn into scale. The use of rain water as a possible answer to the problems of hardness is only advisable in areas where air pollution does not

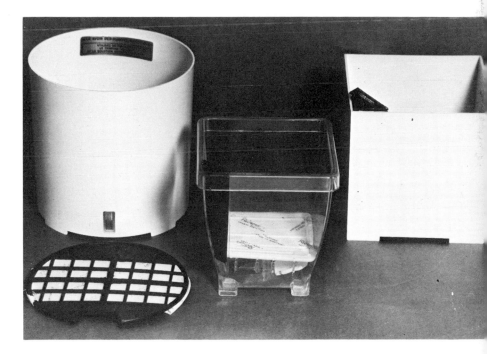

A selection of water supply systems that will convert earth born plants to hydroculture methods.

introduce any harmful materials; even then, note the manufacturers' recommendations about water if you are using an ion exchange fertilizer.

Plants benefit from moisturizing with a spray, because in these days of central heating they often suffer too dry an atmosphere. While impeding plant growth, the dry air is also unpleasant for human beings. In our heavily automated society, there are, of course, moisturizers which make spraying superfluous. Dust should be gently bathed from the leaves with tepid water.

The water and food solution will naturally have to be renewed periodically. This will be necessary more often with larger, fast-growing plants than with the slower-growing specimens and the makers of different fertilizers will suggest the frequency with which it should be done, but on average twice a year will be sufficient to keep the water fresh. If symptoms develop that suggest over concentration of salts or the presence of toxic substances, flush the tank as necessary. A plastic tube with a bulb for squeezing the air out of tube and drawing the water out of the trough can be used as a siphon. One end of the pipe goes through the filling tube into the trough, the other to a bucket, which is at a lower level than the trough. After emptying the trough, refill it with clean tap water and empty again for thorough cleaning. Afterwards, mix clean water and food solution according to the directions on the packet and add through the filling tube until the water level meter reaches maximum height.

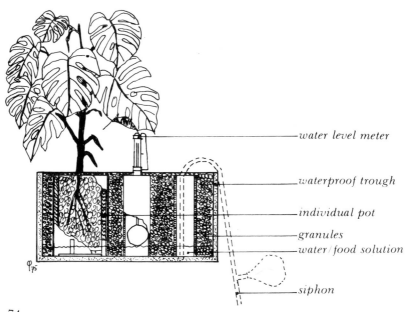

water level meter

waterproof trough

individual pot

granules

water/food solution

siphon

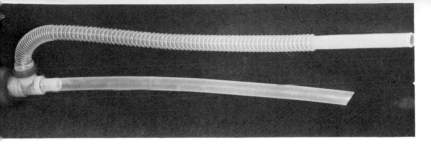

A trough filling syphon.

Ion exchange fertilizers do not have to be renewed, although fresh nutrients must be added at regular intervals. This can be done a few times a year during normal topping up of the water. With this method of feeding, it is particularly important to let the water level reach minimum and remain there for a few days before filling up to allow oxygen to reach the roots and, since the water is not changed, to ensure that as little as possible of the old water is left in the trough.

Owners of large numbers of plants can take out upkeep contracts with hydroculture firms, who will then examine troughs regularly, prune fast-growing plants, tie up climbers, remove yellow leaves, treat diseases and top up water and nutrient solution as necessary. In England, Acorn Nursery run a maintenance service for plants in offices, homes, restaurants, etc. Between their visits, the owners have to take care of the maintenance themselves. It is best for one person to take this responsibility.

Of course, hydroculture troughs are not meant to be used as dustbins. However, in cleaning them one often encounters coffee dregs, cigarette ends and other foreign matter which is not beneficial to plants. The plants may also suffer in positions where people frequently brush against them in walking by.

The things you should look out for during regular inspection of the plants are:

The growing medium—is it too wet for adequate aeration, or too dry? Make sure drainage outlets are not blocked, and remove debris, dead leaves, etc. from the surface. Are the plants looking healthy? If leaves are yellowing, look for deficiencies or over watering; if the plants seem to be wilting, are they too dry, or suffering from overcrowded roots. (Some plants, e.g. tomatoes, are prone to diseases which are characterized by wilting.) Remove dust or dirt from the leaves and tidy up generally, tying and pruning the plants as necessary. Are external conditions as they should be? In hot, dry weather, spray the plants and give them some shade if they need it.

The value of regular care cannot be over stressed—the better you get to know your plants, the more quickly you will spot anything unusual and potentially harmful.

*This thoughtful blend of the colours in trough and plant will enable the
arrangement to live harmoniously with antique or modern furniture alike.*

Light

Although hydroculture is not directly concerned with the subject of light, the increasing tendency to buy large plants, whether grown in water or earth, and scatter them about interiors leads us to the fact that plants need light. In addition, the lack of competition for nutrients and water, which is one of the advantages of hydroculture, makes it possible to grow more plants in a smaller space than could be expected with earth cultivation. For this reason, care must be taken that light is not cut off by overcrowding.

The needs of individual species vary; some plants are light worshippers, others are content with reasonably light shade. A pineapple plant requires a different position from a *Rhododendron* (most frequently known as an Azalea), but any plant which is receiving insufficient light will be spindly and weak, ceasing to flower. New leaves will be small and pale. In still worse light conditions, the plant will probably die from the lack of that all-important source of energy and growth. In nature, sunlight is always present to provide the capacity to carry out the intake and assimilation of feeding material in the process that we term photosynthesis. The plant takes in carbon dioxide from the air by means of microscopically small openings in the skin of the leaf. In the presence of light, with water and diluted nutrients transported through the roots, the carbon dioxide is turned into organic material, sugars for example, while oxygen is released.

When there are a number of plants in the room, the release of oxygen makes for a healthy atmosphere in living room or working area. Artificial light of sufficient strength makes this possible, although the reverse was claimed only a few years ago. Not all the wavelengths available are of the same value to the plants; leaves absorb some in quantity and others hardly at all. Experiments show that the red light appears to encourage growth. Violet on the other hand promotes no great increase in length, but encourages sturdy growth. As a preponderance of red light causes weak, spindly growth, a good combination of rays from the whole spectrum is necessary—that is to say red, orange, yellow, green, blue, indigo and violet light.

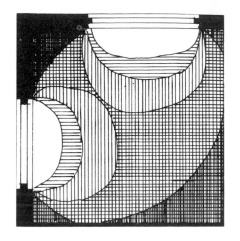

A floor plan view of
light intensity
produced by 2 windows
in a room 4 x 5 meters
(12 ft. x 15 ft.)

 90-100%
ideal

 70-90%
very good

50-70%
good

30-50%
medium

10-30%
bad

 —10%
growth cease

A cross section view of
the light intensity from
one window

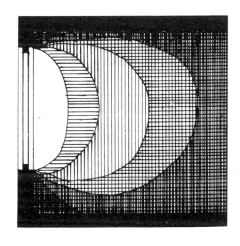

Calculating light intensity

In temperate countries, at the height of summer, the light intensity at noon is about 100,000 Lux. In the shade, the level drops to 10,000 Lux. In the months of March and September, at three o'clock in the afternoon, the sunlight is measured at 25,000 Lux; December sun at the same time of day gives 3000 Lux. These levels of illumination are measured out of doors—on the window sill they will naturally be lower. In the shade near a window on a cloudless day in midsummer, the level will be about 10,000 Lux at noon. One metre further into the room, the light intensity is around 1800 Lux.

If the intensity beside the window is 2000 Lux, then it will be 600 Lux half a metre further into the room and 180 Lux at two metres from the window. Strong, less demanding plants need a basic 800 Lux to grow, and colourful plants rather more—a Cordyline for instance needs 1000-2500 Lux, and a *Saintpaulia* (African Violet) flowers best at 5000 Lux. Of course, every plant's need for light is different. With exceptions, we can distinguish three main groups: a small number of plants which are accustomed to full sunlight, the biggest group, plants which demand full daylight with protection from strong sunlight, and those which live in the shade, needing less

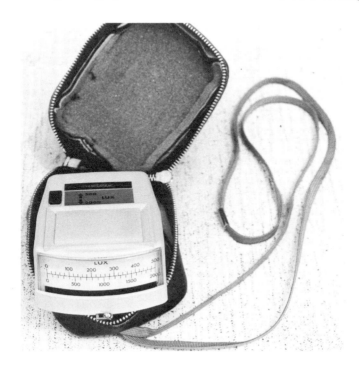

For healthy growth cacti need about 16 hours of light.

light and less able to withstand the sun's rays. Evaporation is another important factor—shade loving plants (ferns) often prefer damp surroundings.

It is essential to measure the amount of light available before deciding on the position of large, forceful plants. A lux meter is needed for accurate measurement.

Which lamps to use

Measurements indicate a deficiency in so many cases that it is often necessary to make use of artificial light to guarantee the best chance of survival for the plants. Lamps with a high radiation output (the amount of electricity that is turned into a useful quantity of light) are preferable. It is often convenient to use several lamps to provide extra light if the plant or trough is in too dark a position.

In choosing the type of lamp, we must consider the amount of light that must be provided, the amount of powder needed, the size of the plant arrangement, the cost of installation, and any incidental demands, such as reflectors and special equipment.

The available lamps include bulbs, fluorescent lights; for a higher output there are, among others, super high pressure mercury or

This tastefully presented Dracaena *would require 13 hours of light to ensure its healthy and vigorous growth.*

mercury iodide lamps, high pressure sodium vapour lamps (all types using 400 Watts) or a 160-Watt mixed light lamp.

Industry and science are still seeking the most efficient illumination for plants, especially now that they are often placed in darker positions than the window sill. Whatever installation you choose, the strength of radiation should be distributed as evenly as possible over the plants. To achieve this, the lamps should be positioned at the appropriate distance from the plants—for a fluorescent light with two 40-Watt tubes, this would be 16-32 in. (40-80 cm.) away.

For this reason, it is often unsatisfactory to hang lights from the ceiling. The height has to be varied according to the desired strength of radiation, and the distance between lamp and plants has to maintained in a fixed ratio with the level of light produced. Certainly, scorching will result if the lamps are too close to the plants.

Rest periods of darkness are essential, but the lamps must burn for a sufficient length of time—at least 12 hours and often longer for the best results. A Dracaena needs about 13 hours, and a Dieffenbachia or cactus as much as 16 hours.

Many plants in offices, and living rooms, for that matter, fail to grow well; they look sickly and may have yellow leaves. It is usually

Codiaeum *(Croton) needs about 2500 Lux*

not that they are too wet, or too dry, or that the system of hydroculture has gone wrong. They *may* need more nutrients or be otherwise unwell, but the seedy look most often results from insufficient light.

How much light is needed?

All plants need a certain amount of light. The list shows the basic requirements of the best known indoor plants—in many cases even more light is better.

Aechmea (Bromeliaceae)	1000 Lux
when in flower	2500 ,,
Aglaonema	1000 ,,
Ananas (Pineapple)	1500 ,,
Anthurium	1000 ,,
when in flower	2500 ,,
Aphelandra	2500 ,,
when in flower	5000 ,,
Begonia	2500 ,,
when in flower	5000 ,,
Billbergia	1000 ,,
when in flower	2500 ,,
Cacti	2500 ,,
when in flower	5000 ,,
Chamaedora	1000 ,,
Chlorophytum	1000 ,,
Cissus	1000 ,,
Clivia	1000 ,,
when in flower	5000 ,,
Codiaeum (Croton)	2500 ,,
Cordyline	1000 ,,
Cryptanthus	1000 ,,
Cyperus	1000 ,,
Dieffenbachia	1000 ,,
Dizygotheca	1000 ,,
Dracaena	1000 ,,
Fatshedera	800 ,,
Fatsia	800 ,,
Ficus	1000 ,,
Guzmania	1000 ,,
when in flower	2500 ,,
Hedera (Ivy)	800 ,,
Hoya (Wax Plant)	2500 ,,
when in flower	5000 ,,

Maranta (Prayer Plant)	800	,,
Neoregelia	800	,,
Nephrolepis (Sword Fern)	800	,,
Nidularium	1000	,,
Pandanus	2500	,,
Peperomia	2500	,,
Philodendron	800	,,
Scindapsus (Ivy Arum)	800	,,
Sansevieria	1000	,,
Saxifraga (Mother of Thousands)	1000	,,
Schefflera	1000	,,
Spathiphyllum	800	,,
when in flower	2500	,,
Syngonium	800	,,
Tradescantia (Wandering Jew)	1000	,,
Vriesia (when in flower)	1000	,,
Yucca	2500	,,
Zebrina	1000	,,

Prevention of disease

Plants are often susceptible to disease and parasitic attack, although for many of them the conditions of hydroculture are ideal, and the risks are lower than with plants grown in earth.

The causes of disease are often hard to establish. Poor nutrition, insufficient light, the presence of draughts or air that is too dry can all contribute. By plant diseases, in the widest sense of the word, we mean everything that affects the internal and external structure of the plant to such an extent that its development is clearly impaired. Such disorders also appear to engender others. They often attack the plant internally, later producing external symptoms, which may be local (rust, for example) or spread throughout the plant (like mildew).

The creatures responsible for parasitic attacks are always visible on the outside of the plant. Sap-suckers insert sharp mouthparts into the plant tissues, causing discoloration and eventually killing the plant. Always found at points of growth, where the sap is most plentiful, they include aphids, fruit fly, red spider mites, scale insects and thrips, and are usually smaller than the pests like beetles, slugs and the extreme case of locusts, which chew plants, sometimes causing extensive damage very quickly. Other diseases can be caused by fungi, which are parasitic in action, bacteria or viruses. Treatment often takes the form of sprays; some simply kill organisms which eat or touch them, others, described as systemic, are absorbed by the plant, effectively making it poisonous to sap-suckers, etc., for a period of two to three weeks. Many species of common pests like warm, humid living conditions. Others, in contrast, flourish in the kind of warm, dry environment found in centrally heated rooms.

Most of the diseases can be prevented by careful treatment of the plant, maintaining humidity in the air, cutting out draughts, and providing a good position with plenty of light. A good supply of food and water is important: this is already provided in hydroculture. Healthy plants can offer greater resistance against diseases. We can help by maintaining the best possible conditions, paying particular attention to cleanliness. Dirt always encourages the spread of disease; dust and debris should be regularly removed, flies and

85

vermin should be discouraged, and any affected plants which cannot be cured should be taken away and if possible burned.

Nevertheless, in spite of all good care, plants can still be affected by some kind of disease or harmful parasites from external sources. When diseases do break out, control is really a matter of common sense. In preventing or fighting a light infection, results can be achieved by chemical means to which there is only a light risk attached. Nevertheless, no single product is entirely harmless to the user's family and pets or the environment at large. Every method of control, even if it is not highly poisonous (the products based on pyrethrin fall into this category), is a biologically active material which will inevitably produce an effect in other organisms than the one against which it is used. With hydroculture, be aware of the danger that drops of chemicals falling on the substratum may contaminate the water and food solution. The plant then takes in water, nutrients and the chemical, in theory becoming poisonous itself. One can never escape the responsibility of balancing the advantages and disadvantages.

However, government regulations compel makers of insecticides to list the constituents of their product, and all their instructions should be scrupulously followed in the use of these chemicals. Reliable treatments for disease can be obtained from most retail outlets concerned with horticulture. A publication obtainable from Her Majesty's Stationary Office in the UK lists the government-approved products and will give you a chance to judge what is available.

Hydroculture out of doors

The effect of rainwater in diluting the nutrient solution makes hydroculture less of a practicable proposition in the garden. Excess rainwater can be drained out of the trough, but it is more difficult to find a means of maintaining the right level of nutrients in the water. Nevertheless, more and more growers are raising small crops in their garden containers, quite successfully. Shelter should be provided in case of heavy or prolonged rain, which tends to disturb light growing media like vermiculite; if the medium becomes too closely packed it is a simple matter to loosen it with a rake. Dry feeding with nutrient powder is often recommended in long periods of rain. Shelter can easily be made to protect seedlings or tender plants against the full force of sun, rain or wind. If you need to stake tall plants which are growing in a lightweight medium, secure the stakes outside the trough or they will simply blow over, probably damaging the plants in the process. Experiments are being carried out, particularly by Luwasa, in the development of outdoor troughs.

Even now, the planting of conifers and garden plants under cover, as often happens in Germany and Switzerland is opening up completely new possibilities in the cultivation of plants for purely decorative purposes, especially at a time when architects are designing more covered shopping streets and play areas, Shoppers derive greater enjoyment from lush greenery grown under hydroculture than a few miserable plants in tubs where the earth has not had any water for weeks. Hydroculture troughs can be placed in covered roof gardens without too much difficulty. This kind of gardening 'out of doors' can help to enhance the environment a little, even though the greenery is artificially created.

Vegetable growing for amateurs

In a time of rising prices and a growing interest in self-sufficiency, people are naturally coming round to the idea of growing their own vegetables. The advantages of hydroculture, which include economical use of water and fertilizers, as well as effort and space, make it well worth considering as a means of cultivation, especially in a small garden where room is limited and the earth may need a lot of attention if it is not to become worked out.

Care should be taken in choosing a suitable nutrient mixture for vegetable growing. Phostrogen is among the ones which are both safe to use and widely available in the UK. Ion exchange fertilizers are *not* suitable.

The ease with which vegetables can be grown depends on the particular requirements of their species. All of them respond to the ready supply of nutrients in balanced quantities, particularly those which are enthusiastic feeders, like cabbages, aubergines and asparagus, and since juiciness is a quality looked for in most of them the ready supply of water is an advantage. Many crops benfit from the cleanliness of the growing medium, especially celery, leeks, etc., which are often hard to prepare for eating when grown in earth.

As a crop which has been the subject of much research in the field of hydroculture, and one which presents a number of difficulties when grown conventionally in earth, tomatoes have attracted a lot of interest. Detailed information on their cultivation can be obtained from several books, including *Tomato Growing Today* by Ian G. Walls. Their needs include a warm growing temperature, regular irrigation (because growth can be seriously impaired by wilting through lack of water) and sufficient space and depth of growing medium in which to develop. They may be grown by any of the methods of hydroculture here described. Alternatively, plastic bags can be bought filled with a growing medium to which nutrients have been added; all you do is insert the plants in slits cut along the plastic when the bag is laid on its side and water regularly. The nutrient film technique, too, is achieving successful results as a method of growing tomatoes commercially. Details are available from the English suppliers of this type of equipment for home use, Barclic Products Ltd.

Good aeration of the growing medium is essential; some crops suffer particularly badly if the medium is insufficiently aerated. These include asparagus, peas and beans, all brassicas and celery. Onions need a dryish medium throughout, but should be allowed to dry off in situ for lifting when they are ripe.

Some plants, like asparagus, which are slow in reaching their full size (asparagus takes three years to begin cropping) can conveniently accommodate another quicker-developing crop between the rows. Lettuces can be planted in seed trays indoors for early growth and transplanted out of doors when the weather is warmer, or they can be sown directly in the spaces between other crops—this gives them the shade they need in hot weather, and they are all the better for quick growing without any setbacks. Do not allow them to sit with their leaves or crowns in water, or rotting may occur. Like lettuce, spinach benefits from rapid development, with a plentiful supply of nitrogen among the nutrients.

In growing any root crop, take care to allow sufficient depth of growing medium—parsnips are extremely deep growing. Radishes naturally need less depth, but must be sown as seed where they are intended to grow, because they react badly to transplanting. Carrots need a light, fairly fine growing medium in which to develop properly.

Flower growing carries with it the special problem of protecting the blooms from wind, rain and, in particularly tender cases, the full heat of the sun. With hydroculture, it is not usually difficult to screen the relatively small areas of plants from the worst of the weather. Tall flowers like gladioli may become top heavy and will certainly need staking.

The special requirements of individual crops are very little affected by the nature of the growing medium whether it be soil or another substratum, as long as conditions are suitable. Details for most types can be found in specialized books.

Continuing research

The methods of hydroculture already developed are valuable in a number of research projects in universities and institutes on the life processes of plants. The results in the field of mineral nutrition in plants are regularly used and adapted. One of the achievements is a universal food solution suitable for many different plants. The research, using radioactive elements which were traced through the plant, went on for six years.

Experts in plant diseases investigated the relationship between mineral nutrition and attacks by insects, moulds and other diseases. At the centre for research into plant physiology (C.P.O.) in Wagenlingen, Netherlands, experiments have been carried out with methods of soilless cultivation and their effects on mineral nutrition. This investigation was not directed towards commercial application.

Abram A. Steiner, head scientific officer, has undertaken with a few co-workers to examine more fundamental questions on this subject. When the decision was taken to end research in the Netherlands, a move was made to put the results into practice in underdeveloped countries, with the idea that the cultivation of plants without earth might alleviate food shortages in those countries. However, we must not expect miracles. The world food organization, F.A.O., is showing considerable interest. It will be very important to give the governments of interested countries objective information about the possibilities and limitations of soilless cultivation. Perhaps the results obtained in Holland and other countries may find practical application in this way, although the problems of food shortage are not going to be solved with peppers, cucumbers and tomatoes alone. Bearing this in mind, experimenters might look for more useful crops for these countries.

Application in infertile regions

Plant cultivation without earth clearly offers excellent opportunities where good soil is not naturally available, or where water is scarce or bad. An example of water culture in an infertile area can be found in the rocky region of Aruba where, on the orders of the government in 1958, cultivation began under the guidance of an American who promised miracles. The project soon failed, and help was sought from Holland in 1961. Within four months of a change in the system, tomatoes, cucumbers and green beans were successfully produced. The intention was to market the produce in Aruba or Curaçao. In the first instance it succeeded, but tomatoes were imported from Venezuela in 1963 for sale at 11 cents a kilo. Production costs in water culture reached 14 cents, partly because of the high price of purified water, and although the Aruban tomatoes were of much higher quality the level of prosperity among the consumers forced them to buy the cheaper tomatoes. The growing of small tomatoes for the preserving industry then became a profitable solution until 1965, when the intended export to New York was prohibited by the United States authorities as a possible source of insect contamination, and production had to come to an end in 1967.

The potential market naturally determines commercial success to a large extent, and there appear to be fewer possibilities for water culture in underdeveloped areas. The level of prosperity is unfortunately too low to guarantee a reasonable sale and the most important needs are instant nourishment, such as grain and rice. Only when there is a chance of export to a more prosperous country can water culture offer realistic financial advantages.

This is the position in the Canaries, where good water is scarce and much of the land relatively infertile. Abram A. Steiner started giving advice there on water culture in 1966. Now several hectares are devoted mainly to the growing of cucumbers and sweet peppers, with production almost exclusively in the winter months. The cucumbers and peppers nearly all find their way to England, Germany and Holland. The water is distilled seawater and therefore fairly expensive.

To achieve good results with water culture, it is necessary to have reliable analyses of food solutions and evaluation of their effectiveness. Help came in the first instance from the analytical laboratory in Las Palmas, but in 1971, on the advice of Abram Steiner, modern laboratory facilities were provided for the analysis of nutrient solutions and evaluation of water.

Progress is also being made in other countries. We find that in the Ukraine, where the soil is more or less infertile, 45% of the crops depend on water culture. This is echoed in Russia as a whole, particularly in recent years—by 1974 about 1000 hectares were already given up to the system.

Attractive hydroculture arrangements soften the harshness of a reception area.

International workgroup in hydroculture

Through the years, an independent non profit making organization has been formed with the aim of promoting water culture throughout the world. This organization, with Abram Steiner as secretary, is called I.W.O.S.C. (International Working Group on Soilless Culture) and gives information on many of the problems that arise.

Members exchange experiences, for example during the international congresses which take place every three to four years. Reports are then written and distributed among members. International courses are held at the laboratories in the Canaries, where interested people and researchers who want to make special investigations into hydroculture are catered for. Normal members have to be actively employed in water culture, either in research and information, or as growers. Congresses are held in various European countries.

Index

List of varieties grown, commercially or tested throughout Europe and Scandinavia

Abutilon hybrid
Aechmea fasciata Bilbergia rhodocyanea
Agave and Aloe
Amaryllis
Aphelandra squarrosa
Bromeliads in a wide range of varieties, including all Cryptanthus species, Guzmanias, Neoregelias, Nidularium, Tillandsias and Vriesias
Bilbergia nutans
Calathea in variety
Clivia miniata
Coleus hybrids
Columnea gloriosa and other varieties of Columnea
Crassula varieties
Crossandra
Cyperus, all varieties
Ferns in variety, including Adiantum, Asplenium nidus, Blechnum Gibbum, Nephrolepis, Platycerium, Polypodium, Pellaea and Pteris
Fatshedera lizei
Grevillea robusta
Haemanthus albiflos
Hedera canariensis Gloire de Marengo
Hedera helix all varieties
Hippeastrum
Hoya carnosa
Hoya bella
Hyacinth
Hydrangea macrophylla
Hydrangea paniculata
Impatiens walleriana
Impatiens New Guinea hybrids
Kalanchoe blossfeldiana and other varieties
Maranta leuconeura kerchoveana and massangeana
Nerine
Nerium oleander
Ornithogalum cordatum
Palms in variety
Pandanus veitchii
Pandanus falcatus
Pandanus sanderi
Pandanus utilis
Parthenocissus inserta
Passiflora caerulea
Passiflora racemosa
Peperomias in variety
Philodendrons in wide variety
Pileas in variety
Piper ornatum
Pisonia brunonianum variegatum Heimerliodendron
Rhoeo spathacea
Saxifraga stolinifera earlier known as S. sarmentosa
Scindapsus pictus
Sparmannia africana
Spathiphyllum floribundum
Sprekelia formosissima
Stenotaphrum secundatum
Stephanotis floribunda
Vallota speciosa
Veltheimia capensis

Vriesia splendens and other varieties — grow well and flower freely in hydro. See Bromeliads
Zantedeschia aethiopica
Zebrina pendula

Cactii and Succulents
Cephalocereus senilis
Ceropegia woodii
Chamaecereus clistocactus
Crassula in variety
Echeverias
Echinocactus
Echinocereus
Echinopsis
Epiphyllums
Euphorbia millii
Gymnocalycium
Mammillarias in variety
Mesambryanthemum
Notocactus
Brasilcactus
Opuntia
Rebutia
Rhipsalidopsis
Rhipsalis
Rochea falcata
Selenicereus grandiflorus
Stapelia
Zygocactus formerly known as Epiphyllum

Orchids
Brassia
Cattleya
Coelogyne
Dendrobium
Epidendrum maybe this is now called Encylcia
Laelia
Lycaste
and Orchids generally

Epiphytic or Tree Orchids
such as Coelogyne cristata
Dendrobium
Epidendrum
Laelia
Lycaste
Miltonia
Odontoglossum
Phalaenopsis and so on

Terrestrial or Ground Orchids
such as Paphiopedilum

List of Houseplants grown in Hydroculture by Rochfords either on a commercial scale or tested by them for eventual commercial growing

Adiantum fragrans
Aglaonema Silver Queen
Ananas bracteatus striatus
Aglaonema roebelinii
Anthurium andreanum
Anthurium crystallinum
Anthurium hookeri